When God gives hope through Jesus, the Holy Spirit, and others. Stories of being seen with a compassionate and listening heart.

A
Gentle
Courage

Barbara Robbins-Ripps

WESTBOW
PRESS®
A DIVISION OF THOMAS NELSON
& ZONDERVAN

WestBow Press books may be ordered through booksellers or by contacting:

WestBow Press
A Division of Thomas Nelson & Zondervan
1663 Liberty Drive
Bloomington, IN 47403
www.westbowpress.com
1 (866) 928-1240

Scriptures taken from the Holy Bible, New International Version®, NIV®.
Copyright © 1973, 1978, 1984, 2011 by Biblica, Inc.™ Used by permission
of Zondervan. All rights reserved worldwide. www.zondervan.com The
"NIV" and "New International Version" are trademarks registered in
the United States Patent and Trademark Office by Biblica, Inc.®

ISBN: 978-1-9736-9749-7 (sc)
ISBN: 978-1-9736-9751-0 (hc)
ISBN: 978-1-9736-9750-3 (e)

Library of Congress Control Number: 2020913135

Print information available on the last page.

WestBow Press rev. date: 07/30/2020

Introduction

Welcome- thank you for spending this time with me. I am a 63-year-old wife, and mom, step-mom, and grandmother. I grew up in San Antonio, Texas. I come from a diverse background of farmers, general store owners, brewery workers, truck drivers, bankers, nurses, and much more. I was employed in the Northside Independent School district as an instructional assistant in the Special Education department for several years. I also ran a registered daycare in my home while my children were young. I worked for the Archdiocese of San Antonio for eleven years as a Director of Religion, Coordinator for middle school and high school, youth ministry in several parishes, and was even a Pre K teacher for a year. I also volunteered in the prison ministry for eight years. It was a medium-security prison. My eyes were opened up to a special group of people. I taught sacramental preparation, shared Jesus, and prayed with the inmates that attended our classes and Mass. God has just blessed me in so many ways by allowing me to get to know many amazing people throughout my lifetime. I can tell you beyond a shadow of a doubt I have seen when someone's heart is touched by Jesus. In the pre-school and prison the look on someone's face is so beautiful and so similar. There are peacefulness and stillness that seems to overcome them. I have seen a very active four-year-old become so still during meditation and then ask if we can do it again. I have seen a room full of prisoners become still and quiet while listening to a Matthew West song and then have several ask the name of the song so they can tell their sons to listen. Amen. I have seen so many faces that have been touched by Jesus and then seen them stand taller and stronger and face life with the Gentle Courage that only comes from Christ.

This book is dedicated to the people God has placed in my life and the gentle courage displayed through them as they met the many challenges of life. The first chapter is dedicated to Jesus. There are so many ways that gentle courage was lived out in His life on earth but I will focus on one that has inspired me and given me the strength to face difficult circumstances in my life.

I pray more than anything that you receive hope and are empowered by the stories of connection to God that give strength beyond words to go forward every day even with the greatest challenges.

The other theme that will be woven through these stories is being seen with compassionate eyes and heard with a listening heart. In our busy world with distractions that are all around and in our pocket in the form of a phone we can become blind, deaf, and have tunnel vision. Our world is so driven by e-mails and the internet that we seldom look at each other in the eye.

When we don't look into someone's eyes we become complacent and distant. We don't see eyes that are sparkling with excitement or saddened with deep pain or isolation.

I invite you throughout this book to reflect on your story and spend some precious time with our Heavenly Father.

My prayers are with you ~ Enjoy the journey recalling sweet and even the painful memories where God was so present.

Be still and know that I am God

Psalm 46:10 NIV

Chapter 1

Jesus

I am with you always

Matthew 28:20 NIV

I am sitting at my table in my prayer room so excited and nervous to begin writing this book and yet filled with anxiety as well. I am doing my best to stay focused on Jesus knowing He is with us.

It is Tuesday, March 31, 2020. Our world is upside down amidst the Covid-19 Virus Pandemic.

We have been quarantined for two weeks in our home. We only go out to grocery shop and we are very careful with gloves and Clorox wipes in hand. The Coronavirus began in China and has now spread throughout the world. Businesses, schools, and restaurants have closed their doors.

It is a scary time for all. Doctors, nurses, and all medical staff risk their lives each day. The military is setting up mobile hospitals and hospital ships on each coast. Even the people who deliver packages and all who keep our grocery stores running are risking their health each day.

So many people have lost their jobs and health insurance and are financially insecure right now.

During this huge worldwide storm there is our hope in Jesus. You can see Jesus' compassion in medical workers all around the world. You can see Jesus in our country as individuals and families pull together and follow the restrictions to end this pandemic. You can also see selfishness in those that take advantage of the situation and try to scam the vulnerable or just outright disregard the restrictions and put so many at risk. There are so many sending texts and messages inviting family and friends to pray with them. There has been so much divisiveness in our world and now you see so many coming together to end this crisis. I intended to begin this book differently but with our current situation I could not leave this out. The stories I am going to share are about people in my life that made a huge impact on me. Now in these uncertain times, we are facing, Jesus is the Lighthouse in the storm. Every day in our nation and throughout our world there are millions of individuals who are that Light for others. One person reaching out makes all the difference in the world. My heart aches watching so much death and uncertainty and at the same time beats with such hope as I see so many heroes risking it all for others. That is the message that I wish to share in this book. I will honor the individuals that have made such an impact on my life, and I invite you to remember those special individuals in your life as well.

I will begin with my very best friend, Jesus. I was sitting in my first- grade class in a Catholic school when I profoundly met Jesus. My teacher's name was Sister Bernadette. She was young and full of love for God and her first- grade class. She extended that love to us each day. I was very shy and quiet when I began school. I was so excited to learn everything and so grateful for the peaceful setting of the classroom and the church. My home life had many ups and downs and was sometimes filled with turmoil. This peaceful setting gave me comfort and a feeling of security. There will be a theme throughout this book that will be revealed in each chapter. It is the great pain of feeling invisible and the great joy of being seen and feeling of value.

The scripture at the beginning of this chapter is "I am with you

Always', Matthew 28:20 NIV. Sister Bernadette taught me that Jesus is with us in every situation. That is one of the greatest gifts I have ever received. She also demonstrated to me what Jesus was like through her actions. You never forget the kindness that just envelops your heart and changes your world. It changed my life from being lonely at times to know the comfort of a friend each day through my teacher. One day I became sick at weekly Mass in the middle of the church. Sister Bernadette swept me in her arms and rushed me to the restroom. She washed my face with cold water and simply cared for me. I felt her concern and kindness. It meant so much to me that I keep it as a treasured memory. (Kind of silly, spitting up in church is one of my most treasured memories, but it is!)

Sister Bernadette taught us about the special presence of Jesus in the Eucharist. She taught us that Jesus is with us in the Eucharist to give us the strength to be able to go out and share that kindness with others who are in need. While we prepared to receive our sacraments she taught us about this loving, forgiving man we know as Jesus. Jesus became real to me. She taught us to extend the love of Jesus to others. In serving others you experience the love of Jesus in such a tangible, real way. She taught us the commandments and that God calls us to live the very best life we can. She taught us about forgiveness and reconciliation when we don't make the right choices. She helped us to build a foundation on God's word. She told us to strive to be holy. I am forever grateful to Sister Bernadette for teaching me to pray. I am so grateful to her for seeing me when I felt lost and invisible.

I moved to the other side of San Antonio in the second grade. Sister Bernadette and I wrote letters to each other for almost 20 years. Later in life we lost contact with each other for a while, but never in our hearts. Just as Jesus is with me always, she is with me as well. She asked our class to please pray for her each time we take communion and I did. She taught me about Jesus and she showed me through her actions who he was. She made me feel valued when I felt lost. I believe that is what Jesus did for so many when he walked this earth. I know that throughout this life Jesus has shown His love for me through others, in a song, in a sunset that takes my breath away, and in quiet moments we share near a flowing river or gazing at a majestic mountain. I felt Him when holding my children's little hands and hugging them tightly.

Throughout my life I loved sharing Jesus with others. I loved teaching Sunday school classes and then teaching my children's classes. I loved working for God at home, in the church, in our family, and in the prison system. In my late 40's and early 50's, I was a volunteer in the Prison Ministry. I taught a class from the book entitled "Believing in Jesus" by Leonard Foley, O.F.M.i

I opened the class up to inmates from all religious faiths. It was an awesome experience. We grew from a class of 9-10 to a class of 30-40 inmates at times. It was such an awakening for me to see a room full of fallen men reaching out to God and open to change. Don't get me wrong, it wasn't always an easy class to teach especially being a woman. There was respectfulness that I felt from most but I had several inmates that worked at challenging me. That was all part of the experience. It always is. There are always challenges. But when Jesus and redemption are the themes there is always enlightenment. I shared with them and they shared so, so, much with me. What a Blessing! One of the most important lessons I was led to share with them was the lesson I feel Jesus was sent to share with us.

The Greatest Commandment

Hearing that Jesus had silenced the Sadducees, the Pharisees got together. One of them, an expert in the law, tested him with this question: Teacher, which is the greatest commandment in the Law?

Jesus replied: "'Love the Lord your God with all your heart and with all your soul and with all your mind.' This is the first and greatest commandment. And the second is like it: 'Love your neighbor as yourself.' All the Law and Prophets hand on these two commandments."

Matthew 22:34-40 NIV

I shared with the inmates that when life sets choices before you ask yourself two questions,

1. Am I Loving God?
2. Am I Loving others?

> It is so simple and yet so very difficult at times. We call on the Holy Spirit in these difficult times.

The following scripture from Matthew has given me the courage in my adult life at times to remain silent when I could speak up to defend myself. I saw Jesus remain silent and let his life speak for him.

Jesus before the Sanhedrin

Those who had arrested Jesus took him to Caiaphas the high priest, where the teachers of the law and the elders had assembled. But Peter followed him at a distance, right up to the courtyard of the high priest. He entered and sat down with the guards to see the outcome.

The chief priests and the whole Sanhedrin were looking for false evidence against Jesus so they could put him to death. But they did not find any, though many false witnesses came forward.

Finally, two came forward and declared, "This fellow said, 'I am able to destroy the temple of God and rebuild it in three days.'"

Then the high priest stood up and said to Jesus, "Are you not going to answer? What is the testimony that these men are bringing against you?" But Jesus remained silent.

The high priest said to him, "I charge you under oath by the living God: Tell us if you are the Messiah, the Son of God."

"You have said so, "Jesus replied." But I say to all of you: From now on you will see the Son of Man sitting at the right hand of the Mighty One and coming on the clouds of heaven."

Then the high priest tore his clothes and said, "He has spoken blasphemy! Why do we need any more witnesses? Look, now you have heard the blasphemy. What do you think?" "He is worthy of death," they answered. Then they spit in his face and struck him with their fists. Others slapped him and said, "Prophesy to us, Messiah. Who hit you?"

Matthew 26:57-68 NIV

This scripture has inspired and led me through some of the most difficult times in my adult life. Jesus was accused but stayed silent. Jesus let his life speak for him. Then with great courage, A

GENTLE COURAGE, Jesus spoke the truth. Peter, one of the closest people to Jesus did not stand up for him. There was great suffering. In the end life on earth as Jesus knew it ended but resurrected life began. I can't even count how many times I have felt Jesus' resurrection power.

How can I explain in words the friend I have had in Jesus? He has been by my side through it all.

When I wanted so badly to just give up he would give me the strength to go on. It would be an inspiration through a song, through a person, in a sunset, or through His Word. Sometimes it was when someone would make me so upset that I knew I had to stand tall and move forward with Jesus right by my side. There are times when I do not doubt that the person sharing hopeful words had no idea of the struggle I was facing. The Holy Spirit prompted them to send a song or scripture and there was my sign again not to give up and that God's got this. Amazing!

How do you put AWE into words? There have been times when I have been prompted to visit or text someone and they respond with the question, "How did you know I needed that right now"? The answer is that I didn't. God did! And I'm so glad I listened. Even in times when I feel down and argue a bit with God that I just don't have it in me right now He lifts us both up in the connection. God is good! All the time!

Have there been times in your life when you had to do what was right even though it brought you great pain? Have there been times when you had to remain silent because no one would listen anyway?

Have there been times when you had to stand up and speak the truth for someone or yourself?

There is always that hope and promise of resurrected life. Sometimes we experience many resurrected moments throughout our lives. Thank you to my friends Bonnie, Elena, Juanita, Sharon, Clare, Raeleene, Marisol, and Missy for helping me through those resurrection years. Through shared faith, friends, and Bible studies God gives us New Life.

Reflection Page

This chapter touched on a few special moments in my relationship with Jesus.

I would like to invite you to take some time to reflect on times you have felt the presence of Jesus in your life.

_____

_____

_____

_____

_____

_____

_____

_____

_____

_____

_____

_____

Chapter 2

My Parents

"Honor your father and your mother, so that you may live long in the land the Lord your God is giving you."

Exodus 20:12 NIV

The next chapters will be written in chronological order. They will not include all of the people I have been blessed to know with gentle courage but many. I consider everyone I have known to be a blessing and a lesson.

The first two people I was blessed to have in my life were my parents. I will remind you that I am 63 years of age so there is a lot of reflection here. When I was young I called my father "Daddy" and my mother "Mama". I was raised in San Antonio Texas and I was a country girl.

I still call my father "Daddy" and in my teens and older I called my mother "Mom" or "Mary".

My mom passed away in 2005. She had early-onset Alzheimer's disease.

Growing up in our household was not always easy. I think most of us can probably say that there were challenges in our families. That is life. There was love, pain, sickness, love, happiness, sadness, fun, pain, love, and on and on. I want to honor my parents in the truth that even when life is complicated it can be wonderful when God is at the center.

As I mentioned in the first chapter there was turmoil in our home when I was young. My dad drank a lot and my mother had bipolar disorder. They both had issues to deal with and there were ups and downs in life but my brothers and I still knew that they loved us. That was a blessing.

Sister Bernadette taught us the commandments. She taught me to honor my father and mother. As I grew older I learned that that did not mean to always agree with them but to honor them. This was an important lesson for me.

The reason I am being so real is that I want to encourage others to look at their circumstances as opportunities to build God's Kingdom. I know some circumstances are completely out of our control. I know that some have no parents to reminisce about. I am just asking you to look for God. Look for that gentle hand, smile, or nod coming from a person of honor in your life. In some circumstances if that is even difficult to do remember a time when you were that person for someone else. If all else fails remember when Our Heavenly Father was there for you, even if you didn't feel it at the time.

There were many years that life was tough. People on the outside didn't realize all that went on within our home. My parents were kind to the family and our friends. There were the internal struggles that as a young person made life difficult at times. We always put up a good front. My cousin Dorothy has a saying that I love, "They were doing the best they could at the time". This is so true. We all have issues that are out of our control sometimes. My mom had a chemical imbalance that she had to manage with medication. My dad learned later in life to manage and eventually stop drinking. These changes helped him to stabilize his diabetes and bring so many changes to his life and our family. How many times can we say that for ourselves? I did the very best I could at the time… considering the circumstances.

My dad took us on vacation to Junction and Medina Lake. He taught us to swim and to fish and the value of spending time with family and friends. He provided for our family. Later in life he was always helping the elderly in our family. My great Aunt was always included on our fishing trips. Maybe we were included on her trips! My dad would help the older members of his family with lawn work, or take food to them when they couldn't get out. He was there to help out family and friends whenever he could.

My mom made sure that we went to church every Sunday. She prepared Sunday dinners and invited my grandmothers and great aunt to dinner because they were widowers. She cooked and cleaned and tried to attend the events we were in at church and school. These are the memories that I hold on to. The ones I see God in. I also see God in difficult times. I have two brothers and we were very close. We stuck together to get through the difficult times. We were there for each other. God was with us when there were arguments between my parents late at night. God got us through some rough situations.

My parents were so excited to be grandparents. Their hearts softened and they were so tickled with those grandbabies. My parents went through many changes after that. My mom was hospitalized many times. My brother Robie passed away at the age of 39 from massive hemorrhage in his brain stem. My parents grew closer after his passing and tried to be there for each other. When I was 41 they sat down at their kitchen table and told me they were sorry for the past. My Mom told me she was sorry that I always had to be the adult. I think after my brother passed away so suddenly they realized that life is precious. There was reconciliation and there was love. I see gentle courage throughout their lives. Courage to keep trying. Courage to keep loving.

My mom loved being a grandmother! She had a great sense of humor. She was diagnosed with early-onset Alzheimer's when she was in her early sixties. Several years later my dad and I shared the responsibility of caring for her in our homes 3-4 days at a time. Eventually we placed her in a Care Center. Her doctor had recommended this and after months of sleepless nights where she wandered through our homes, we agreed we had no choice. My brother Shorty was wonderful in making the arrangements with my dad. I was having a hard time the first day she resided there. I had purchased a new bed cover and pictures for the wall and was trying to make her comfortable. I kept playing with the lights in the room and ask her if they were okay and her response was, "Oh Barbara, My lights have been out for years!" She made me laugh and relieved the tension in the room. That is a Gentle Courage. Even during sickness and change she dared to make things easier. She made us laugh. What a great comfort. My point...Try to keep your sense of humor. Smile often. It is a saving grace.

We had amazing doctors and caregivers that helped my Mom. We had doctors we had to let go because they just wanted to fill her with more and more medications. God was with us when we had to stand up for her. God was with us when we found great new doctors who helped her live out the next few years in the best way she could.

My dad did the same. My mom passed away in 2005. He has continued to try to be there for the family. He was very independent for years. We have our holiday celebrations at his house and that has allowed his grandchildren and great-grandchildren to have a very special relationship with him. He just needs a ride and some assistance now. My brother Shorty gets him to doctor appointments and fixes a few things around the house. We are trying to be there as we watched our parents caring for their family years ago. I see that Gentle Courage in my dad. He is lonely but he keeps going for himself and his family. It is such a blessing. He has shared with me that he hopes God will allow him to join my mother someday.

My Dad and Mom always helped out the elders in our family. They included them in outings, dinners, and vacations. They mowed their yards and took them food when they needed it. I think that is one of the greatest lessons they taught us. They taught us not only to help out with things others need but to sit and visit with them and enjoy their company. They are a treasure.

This story is so abbreviated. My point is we all have a story. We all have had challenges but with God we keep going! We welcome more grandchildren and great-grandchildren in our world.

I want to thank my parents from the bottom of my heart for all the love they showed me, my brothers, and our family through the years. This is another moment when words don't express how deeply we feel. We made many amazing memories together. We made it through the rough times. We made it through with God, and with a grateful heart.

Do the best that you can with what you have at the time...
Remember to honor others
Even in the difficult times
Stand up for yourself
Stand up for others

Go to God with all your concerns
Forgive
Move Forward

Reflection Page

Chapter 3

My Children

Shannon   Brianne   Dusty

Evaristo   Daniel   Bonnie

I thank my God every time I remember you. In all my prayers for all of you, I always pray with joy because of your partnership in the gospel from the first day until now, being confident of this, that he who begins a good work in you will carry it on to completion until the day of Christ Jesus.

Philippians 1:3-6 NIV

How in the world do you put into words the love you feel for your children? When I paused to think about which scripture I would choose for this chapter it came to me quickly. I thank my God every time I remember you. My girls are in their early forties and my son is in his late thirties. My sons-in-law are in their forties and my daughter-in-law in her thirties. Wow does the time go by fast! My children have blessed me with many grandchildren the oldest being twenty-one and the youngest one-month-old. The love that I have for my children started the day I found out I was pregnant.

I was so excited anticipating their birth and preparing a place for them in this world.

The gentle courage begins almost immediately after you bring them home. You swaddle them in soft blankets so they feel secure and will maybe stay asleep for a few hours so you can take a nap. Soon they gather enough courage to stay in their crib overnight. Then it isn't long they are bravely taking their first steps. After that watch out! They are off to the races and hard to keep up with.

It is a joy and so exciting to watch every milestone they accomplish. It is awesome to see the bond that they form and how much they love each other. It melted my heart when I saw them reach out to other little children with kindness. It broke my heart when I witnessed someone hurting them. When they reached middle school and adolescents it takes gentle courage on the parent's part to remember this child (that looks a lot like yours, but acts like an alien) will return after the moon orbits around the earth about thirty-nine times. (three years LOL)

I am so very proud of my three children. They are loving, kind, Faith-filled individuals with servants' hearts. They are all blessed to be married to loving spouses as well.

I don't want to reflect on sad times in our life but it is at these times I see the strength God has given us to get through. I want to express to my children how their gentle courage during divorce in our lives was beyond courageous. I want to tell all children that have been through a divorce that your hearts are special and we know that your experience was so difficult.

My children were strong and loving and broken all at the same time. I am so sorry that children bear so much pain during these times of loss. The good news is that even going through such deep loss, with God, they were able to move forward. Was it difficult? Yes it was. Are there scars? Yes there are. But they are three strong adults who have compassion and a spirit of Love that they share with others knowing their pain. There are many children that go through this life with such an act of amazing gentle courage as well. There are so many that have lost a parent to death, military separation, absence of a parent that is incarcerated, or maybe in a foster or adoption situation. Many of these children tap into the strength and courage they are given by God. There are many abandoned and abused children in our world. I attended a concert by a group of young people from another country that were on their own after losing their parents and all family members to war. I was so inspired by their performance and their smiles. They had been taken in by an American couple who started a school and built a church and home for these children. Their music was truly inspired by God and they beamed when they shared their testimonies of how God had saved their lives. I was going through a difficult time personally and after hearing their testimonies I knew that I needed to stand tall and keep walking with God. Again and again the message of this chapter and this book is that with God and each other we can make it through.

I see the gentle courage displayed by my children every day. Shannon and Evaristo have full- time jobs, a house full of children, and are active in ACTS retreats in their church and serve God in many ways. Brianne and Danny work very hard in their positions in their companies, take care of their three children, and serve God on ACTS teams and other ministries in their church. Dusty and Bonnie work very hard, are raising their three boys, and are serving in their church communities on ACTS teams and other ministries. I am so grateful for the courage they show in their lives every day. They have tough work schedules, challenges, children's sports schedules, special school events, church ministry schedules, and they just keep on going. They are grateful to God and are strong enough to share their faith with others. Sometimes a devotional sitting on your desk or a moment of blessing before you eat your meals can be an opening for conversation for someone who is struggling and needs someone of faith to talk to. Am I being boastful? No. I am praising God for His presence in my children's lives and being grateful for His strength during the difficult times. Currently in our world during the Coronavirus pandemic we are all staying at home separated by miles but all connected in prayer. God is good! I can't imagine how difficult it would be if we didn't share our love for God and each other.

There is not enough time or paper to write about all the times that God has seen us through as a family and as individuals. We have been through many trials and celebrated many joys…together. Our lives are crazy and busy but we text when we need prayers for others or ourselves and we feel the power of God in those shared prayers.

I have seen so many faces that have been touched by Jesus and watch that person stand taller and stronger to face life with the gentle courage that comes from Christ.

I watched my children face so many challenges and get through with the strength that comes from Jesus Christ. My special thanks to Shannon, Brianne, and Dusty for being there for me. I want to thank your spouses as well. I see Jesus in all of you and I am so proud that you share His Light with others. I want to thank Evaristo, Daniel, and Bonnie for loving my children. This is not a fairy tale. There were years when I worried about them not going to church. I went to my pastor and spoke to him about this and he asks, "Do they believe in God?" I said yes. He said, "then don't worry. It will be okay." As I said before there is not enough paper to write about all our life experiences. But it does have a happy ending!

I have been married three times. It is kind of hard to say the words I have been married three times. When I look back I just thank God for the blessings and look for love.

I have been blessed with stepchildren Tonja, Wendi, and George III from my second marriage. My third marriage blessed me with Clayton and Michelle, Travis and Kristi, Alyssa and Jay, and Weston and Melissa. I wasn't comfortable with the term step-children. I don't know what I would like it to be. One day I looked up the definition of the word step in an old Webster dictionary. It said a single completed movement in walking, dancing, or running. I kind of liked that. I thought you take steps, one at a time, to be in a relationship with the new blessings in your life. That's the way I look at it.

I prayed God would bless me with many grandchildren. He heard that prayer! I am blessed with thirty- two grandchildren. Some biological. They are amazing! In this world they are called to display that gentle courage every day. To be kind is not always the cool thing today. But they are Kind and filled with Faith and Strong! I think it is important to mention them by name.

BECAUSE I LOVE THEM! In chronological order Jasmine, Reyna, Hunter, Isaiah, Ally, Hannah, Dalton, Colten, Gavin, Brody, Logen, Cailey, Abby, Tatym, Owen, Ysabella, Paula, Easton, Jaxon, Fender, Evan, Cole, Marisa, Faith, Cason, Tre, Tenley, Ty, Ali, Lane, Maverick, Gideon

God is Good
We Love God
Jesus is with us always
The Holy Spirit guides us
We Love each other
I thank God for every remembrance of you!!!

Reflection Page

Chapter 4

Special

Look at me with the eyes of your heart

For you created my inmost being; you knit me together in my mother's womb. I praise you because I am fearfully and wonderfully made; your works are wonderful, I know that full well.

Psalm 139: 13-14 NIV

The next few pages will be dedicated to some special people in my life. When I was a senior in high school I signed up for a program called teacher training experience. It was the first three classes of the day and I was allowed to choose which school I would like to work at in Northside ISD. It was a part-time job and allowed me to see if this would be an area I would like to work in after graduation. My best friend Bonnie's mom worked at a school for children with special needs and after visiting with her I decided I would like to work there. Special needs, special education, special abilities, special disabilities, it can all be summed up in one word, special. I had never been around children or adults with special needs before. It opened my eyes and my heart to a whole new world. There was pureness about these individuals. The school I worked in started in early childhood and went up to twenty-one years of age. It ranged from classes with learning disabilities, physical challenges, emotional disorders, and combinations of all three. There was on the job training for individuals that were higher level.

I started as an assistant in the early childhood class. I worked with an elderly teacher, Mrs. Dubberly, who loved her students. I was seventeen years old and was so grateful to work with these students and such a loving teacher. It was love at first sight for me. One little boy had down syndrome and had severe seizures. There was a little four- year- old girl named Tina who had spina bifida that could light up the world with her smile. Wendi had muscular dystrophy and emotional problems. There were several other students in that class with their own "special" qualities. It is difficult to assign names to the many different abilities these children have but "special" fits them all.

Wendi lived with her grandfather. Her mom had abandoned her when she was a baby. Wendi's aunt tried to care for her but she had a baby of her own and would leave Wendi in her crib most of the time. She was fed and kept clean but Wendi was seldom held or nurtured. She eventually went to live with her grandfather. Wendi was non-verbal and needed assistance walking. She loved to be rocked and I would sing an Olivia Newton-John song that was popular at the time, I Honestly Love You, almost every day. (Side note, my singing is not so great but Wendi seemed to love it or at least being non-verbal she never complained.) One day I was ill and absent from work. The next day when I returned, Mrs. Blanchard came up to me and said, "Your little Wendi missed you yesterday. She screamed all morning!" Oh my word! She screamed! It was amazing. Wendi rarely reacted to anything. And she spoke. I scooped my little friend up in my arms and we celebrated. The celebrations in our class were so full of excitement and joy. We celebrated when Tina would climb out of her wheelchair and do stunts on the mat. We celebrated when Tina returned from being hospitalized after having a long seizure in our class. She had to be rushed to the hospital to replace a shunt that she had outgrown and was no longer working properly. We celebrated when John and Brian had a good day with no behavioral problems. We celebrated for different reasons than most but with McDonald's happy meals and cupcakes just like the other children their age. Special children. Special moments.

I also helped in the work center which was for older children, high school to twenty-one years of age. We had a silk screening unit which allowed higher level to lower-level students the opportunity to participate in printing and packaging t-shirts for schools and businesses throughout the school district. There were students with very diverse situations. There was a young lady, Michelle, who was around seventeen years of age and she was a quadriplegic. She was a beautiful, non-verbal young girl who was rolled from one corner of the room to the other in her wheelchair to simply watch whatever activity was going on. She drooled quite a bit and it took two people to carefully change her diaper because she was very fragile. Each day I tried to talk to her and move her all around the room so she would feel included. Sometimes my heart would ache when I would see a very sad and lonely look on her face. One day I went over and bent down next to her face and I told her, "I am so sorry. I'm sorry you have to sit alone most of the time and can't participate." She looked up at me and then I saw tears rolling down her cheeks. She was stuck inside a body that she couldn't move, couldn't control. She was non-verbal and so she made no sounds, but you could see expressions on her face. What a beautiful young girl- trapped. It was sad to see her tears but such a tender moment because I felt she knew that I cared. Special, a special young lady that longed to be noticed and spoken to.

The point that I am trying to make in this chapter is that every person is a gift from God. Each person is fearfully and wonderfully made by God. I pray for respect for everyone. It is so important just to take the time to look into others eyes and acknowledge each other as a person of value. We are all valuable. Take time to give a smile, kind word, or a gentle touch.

These children and adults display gentle courage every day.

Their parents, teachers, and caregivers go forward with gentle courage learning different ways to accomplish tasks every day. Many situations are so involved, complicated, and exhausting. The beautiful part is that in the midst of all this I saw great love. Parents and teachers worked tirelessly for others. Sometimes it took months or years to see growth or success but there was gratitude each day as they moved forward. If you ever get the chance to attend the Special Olympics you will see gentle courage in each athlete. You will see coaches cheering on their students and smiles on each face. The event is won simply by participating. When you watch these individuals participating in soccer or little league baseball it is amazing to see the support from the coaches and the whole team.

Look at the individuals that God places in your life in the eye and listen to them attentively.

Open your eyes to see
Open your ears to hear
Open your heart to Love

We are all on the same team. God's Team.

Reflection Page

_____

_____

_____

_____

_____

_____

_____

_____

_____

_____

_____

_____

_____

_____

Chapter 5

Service

"The King will reply, 'Truly I tell you, whatever you did for one of the least of these brothers and sisters of mine, you did for me.'

Matthew 25:40 NIV

Today is Good Friday, April 10, 2020. As I mentioned in previous chapters we are in quarantine due to the Covid-19 pandemic. We have been isolated for about four weeks and will be for several more and then they will make a decision if it should be extended. It is such a solemn and Holy Day today. My husband Randy and I have been watching the movie Jesus of Nazareth and my heartaches. It aches for my hero Jesus and it aches for the doctors, nurses, EMTs, and all essential personnel in grocery stores and all other areas. Jesus came to this earth to teach us all that every single person is of value. He died for our sins and to give us the hope of eternal life. The values he stood up for rocked the world. He suffered to deliver God's command to love one another. Jesus' teachings gave us hope through forgiveness and new beginnings. If you have faith, go forward and sin no more.

I can see the struggles Jesus endured being lived out in our world today. There are thousands of doctors, nurses, and medical personnel risking their lives to save others. They are desperately trying to slow down and stop the Covid-19 virus that is taking the lives of so many. Jesus was living out the commands of Our Heavenly Father to try to stop the virus of hatred and legalism that was killing so many.

It is so beautiful to see the great displays of love and appreciation during this horrible pandemic. Scientists are scrambling to come up with vaccines and tests. In the center of all this turmoil there is hope. There is hope that even when a person succumbs to the virus and there is death there is Hope of Eternal Life in Heaven. So we all try to do our part, or do we? There are leaders of their churches encouraging their members to attend Easter Sunday services. There are so many religious leaders and faiths including the Catholic Church who are not holding services and providing online services or encouraging worship in your own home in whatever way is possible for you and your family. Jesus said, "Love one another!" This is a command from God. If we love we care for each individual by isolating and not putting others at risk. Today, just the same as over 2000 years ago some are misleading their flocks. The good news is there are many, many heroes. There are men and women who stand up for what is right. They are not always applauded at first, but in the end they will be respected for their courageous actions. Every day we hear encouraging stories of individuals or companies that step out with gentle courage to help relieve the situation.

Jesus' actions and His strength and courage to care for others and give up His life impacted and changed our world. The doctors, nurses, cleaning staff, EMT's, Policemen and women, Firemen, grocery store clerks, bus drivers, and so many others who have lost their lives have deeply impacted our world. The innocent who became ill and died alone because of the isolation restrictions are victims of this virus. The beauty we see is the efforts that hospital employees made to try to connect those who were dying through technology to say their last goodbyes. Their sacrifices will never be forgotten. Our world will forever be changed. Something very important to remember is that these individuals were not alone. Jesus was with them. I believe this with all my heart.

We pray for everyone who has lost their life during this pandemic. We pray for all the innocent people that were just in the wrong place at the wrong time. We pray for all who have lost their jobs and are financially unstable that God will lead them to new employment and grant provision for them and their families. We pray with a grateful heart for the promise of eternal life.

History does repeat itself. My prayer is that we open our hearts and our minds to all the lessons God wants us to learn throughout this storm and when it has passed.

When I think of service I think of my brother Robie who passed away in 1997. He was always there to help others. He wasn't the type to wait for you to ask but he was the kind of person who would think about how he could make your life easier in times of trouble. It has taken much courage for Barbara his wife and his sons Robie and Kylie to keep going. There have been many challenges but with God and family they carry on.

Love God and rely on Him for your strength during uncertain times.

Love your neighbor and reach out in whatever way is possible for you.

Stay the course.

Rest in prayer.

Live in gratitude for the blessings each day.

Express that gratitude when you can.

If we all do our part
We can get through this…
TOGETHER.

I have heard this over and over in the past weeks. Beautiful words. I wonder if that is what Jesus was thinking when He died for us. He showed us how God wants us to live by His actions here on earth. He knew we are not perfect but He told us to try to be. He offered us forgiveness for the times we mess up. He gave us hope of eternal life and the Holy Spirit to give us guidance and strength. Then maybe he thought

> If we all do our part
> We can get through this...
> TOGETHER

Reflection page

Chapter 6

Heroes

Remember your leaders, who spoke the word of God to you. Consider the outcome of their way of life and imitate their faith. Jesus Christ is the same yesterday and today and forever.

Hebrews 13: 7-8 NIV

I feel that our heroes are so important in giving us direction in our lives. Jesus of course is my number one hero. The men and women who are working tirelessly to slow down this pandemic and create tests and vaccines for the Covid-19 virus are true heroes. The love and dedication displayed by so many each day are so inspiring. Our country has become so divided and our society is driven by financial gain and for lack of better term false gods. This last month it seems that what matters is coming to the surface. We are all working together so that someday soon we can give hugs again and visit face to face. We long to put in an honest day of work and make an honest wage. It is another case of history repeating itself. I pray we get back to our core values with the help of our heroes. God bless them all!

I will go back to some of the first heroes in my life. My first-grade teacher, Sister Bernadette, helped me to place my faith in Jesus and encouraged me to have a close relationship with him. When I am drawn to other heroes in my life they have similar qualities of Jesus and they share their love and kindness with others. They are people you can trust and who are consistent in how they relate to others.

My parents were two of my heroes because even with all the challenges of life they helped others and loved their family.

When I began working with Special Education in NISD in San Antonio Lorraine Blanchard, my best friend's mom, became one of my heroes. She loved the special needs students so much and taught them especially in the physical education area how to do the best they could and to enjoy the sports and events they were able to participate in. I was very inspired while working there because so many of the teachers and assistants loved their students. They would just be full of smiles and joy when a student accomplished a new task or skill. The students were heroes as well because even with all the physical and mental challenges they may have there was great determination and effort. It was amazing to watch.

There were also heroes in my church. Father Petsch from the parish and school at St. Vincent de Paul was someone I looked up to. He was always kind and joking with us and made us feel special. I was only in the second and third grade but it made me feel welcome and I felt like I belonged in my school and church. Msgr. Kevin Ryan was another hero in the parish St. Rose of Lima where my children grew up. He was kind and compassionate to everyone and was a true model of Christ living in our pastor. He was approachable and you could count on his truthful direction. It was so important to be able to trust a leader in our church, knowing that he was a person of integrity and compassion. We felt like family, God's family, in our parish. When I was raising my children I knew it was so important for them to know God. The most important role model to have is Jesus. When you see Jesus in others you are attracted to them and want to be friends. It is so important who your children choose to be their friends.

One of my heroes is Abraham Lincoln, the sixteenth President of the United States. Here is another life that was taken as he stood with gentle courage, honor, and conviction for all people. In his second Inaugural address he spoke the following words which are now inscribed on one wall of the Lincoln Memorial in Washington D.C. "With malice toward none; charity for all, with firmness in the right, let us strive to finish the work we are in; to bind the nation's wounds..." Everyone recognizes the name of Abraham Lincoln, but I have many heroes that I don't know by name. They are the men and women in our military who dedicate their lives to defending our freedom. I have several family members that have served in the Army, Navy, and the Air Force. I am so very grateful to them and proud. The heroes of the past, the present and those to come are many times silent heroes. They served and there are no memorials erected for them. They are just as important as the ones with statues and memorials. These individuals hold their stories in their hearts and minds and will never be formally recognized. They are no less of a hero. These men and women devote their lives to the common good. There are no words to express the gratitude that you deserve. God Bless You and your families!

I also think it is so important to have heroes in Sports. I try to encourage my grandchildren to learn and read about these role models in sports. Just like us they are not perfect and have had challenges but their light shines through. In the next few lines you will be reminded of how OLD I am by some of my sports heroes. Tom Landry the coach of the Dallas Cowboys was a great coach. Kurt Warner and Drew Brees are two of my favorite football players. Gregg Popovich the coach of the San Antonio Spurs Basketball team is another favorite. David Robinson, Tim Duncan, Bruce Bowen, and Becky Hammon are great role models on and off the court. I Love the Spurs! Steph Curry and Lebron James are more outstanding role models. I'm sure you and your family have your favorites. Thank goodness for our heroes.

The common thread in all these heroes is Love. Love for God.

Love for one another. Love for our country. Love for a sport. Love that reaches through all barriers and saves all souls. I have been particularly struck by the reporting on the news of the persons released from the hospital after recovering from the Coronavirus. If it is possible there are many doctors, nurses, and staff lining the halls and applauding as a recovered person is wheeled out to meet their family. Also in a beautiful display of respect the people who have died are taken out on stretchers escorted by as many doctors and nurses are available to walk them to their places of rest whether it is a hospital morgue or refrigerated truck. Love, beautiful, gut-wrenching displays of Love.

One of my heroes was my spiritual companion many years ago when I was in the Spiritual director internship at Incarnate Word. She truly saw me and advised me to go to therapy and spiritual direction with her because of all the hurt I internalized through the years. This started a process of healing for me that was truly a gift from God. I was diagnosed with PTSD at the time and coming to terms with what I was dealing with was crucial. It was a busy time of my life and I did not allow myself to truly deal with all I was holding inside. I was raising my children, working full time, helping my parents, and in denial as well. It was the beginning of the process though, and so important. Just a year ago I found myself needing to deal with some of my issues. This was twenty years down the road but I knew I needed to seek help. My niece, Pennie, recommended a therapist named Denise. She has helped me work through different circumstances that are still my triggers. It is important for me to receive spiritual direction as well. She is a new hero of mine. She is direct and caring. Throughout my life, I have been counseled by a few professionals that did not help me at the time. My suggestion to anyone is that if you go to someone and it is not a good fit don't give up. It is important to find someone else if you are in need. There is nothing wrong with trying to find someone else because as in life some of us are just not compatible. I pray for all who need help in sorting out their life to find someone to help them through. I am so proud of public personalities who are truthful and helpful in sharing with others their struggles and how they came to deal with them. No one is perfect. We all have work to do. It is not a disgrace but through God's grace we can find help and be healed.

Max Lucado, the author, is one of my heroes. His books and devotionals have been a constant source of strength for me, my children, and my family and friends. I can't tell you how many copies of his books that I have purchased to share because they made such an impact on me. Thank you for your many years of sharing the Word of God with us all in such relatable language.

What a life! It goes by so fast. It is a blessing to look back on all the memories. It is a good thing when you can look back and mostly just remember Love. Three more of my heroes are my Great Aunt Gladys and my two Grandmothers. They were ladies that lost their spouses and lived twenty-five to forty years alone. They were very important parts of our lives and enriched our family for many years. Life is a gift. I pray for all!

Love is Indespensable

If I speak in the tongues of men or of angels, but do not have love, I am only a resounding gong or a clanging cymbal.

1 Corinthians 13:1 NIV

Reflection Page

_____

_____

_____

_____

_____

_____

_____

_____

_____

_____

_____

_____

_____

_____

Chapter 7

Memories with God

Faith in Action

Now Faith is confidence in what we hope for and assurance about what we do not see. This is what the ancients were commended for.

By faith, we understand that the universe was formed at God's command so that what is seen was not made out of what was visible.

Hebrews 11:1-3 NIV

Today is April 15, 2020. I am sitting at my table in my prayer room glancing out the window on a beautiful day. The leaves in the red oak tree are dancing in the wind. The sun is bright and the air is cool and crisp. I can see our garden from my second-story window that is a sign of new life. At the same time in New York, California, and even in the small town of Castroville where I live the Coronavirus is changing our world. Do I see God in the midst of all this? Yes. I hear of so many people with that gentle courage that God equips us with putting their lives on the line every day. You see great love and sacrifice being displayed by so many. I pray that we open our minds and hearts and we see all that God is revealing.

I am very excited to begin the last chapter. I am writing it praying that whoever reads it will receive hope. That is what God has always done for me. He has given me hope most especially through my relationship with Jesus.

I want to share a special memory of God that gave me new strength and hope.

I was on a five-day silent retreat at Lebh Shomea (from the Hebrew meaning Listening Heart) at the Kenedy Mansion in Sarita, Texas. I was going through a very difficult time in my personal life and feeling emotionally and physically exhausted. My spiritual companion, Beth, suggested I go on this silent retreat. She suggested that I stay for 5 days. The first two and a half days I slept. My room was on the third floor of Sarita Kenedy East (1889-1961) mansion and was her bedroom. Today her home is a silent retreat center owned by the Missionary Oblates of Mary Immaculate, a worldwide Catholic Order. You could see the top of the beautiful Palm trees that lined the front lawn of the mansion from my windows. I was finally able to get restful sleep. On the third day I enjoyed sketching from the balcony and on the front lawn of the beautiful property. It was such a gift because there was no time for such pleasure in my busy life. I was working for the church at the time and raising three children. In the evening I enjoyed a quiet dinner with the other guests and then made my way to the library. I sat on the floor and went through an album of photos and articles about Sarita Kenedy East.

The next morning I knelt in the kneeler she must have used in her bedroom for many years. The indentions in the kneeler gave me a sense of her intense prayerfulness. I felt a spiritual closeness to her as I prayed. The ceilings were very tall and at the top above the kneeler there was a beautiful stained glass window of Jesus in the garden. The sun rose directly into that image and it was breathtaking. Thursday of that week I felt led to write for quite a while. I wrote a children's book that I had felt led to write. I quickly wrote on a legal pad the story I wished to share with my children and grandchildren. This was the first sunny day of the week. It had been cloudy and overcast. I went on a bicycle ride in the afternoon to enjoy the trails and wildlife on the ranch. We were not supposed to use the phone but I kept feeling prompted to call my daughter who was living with me at the time. She was in college and working at Outback. When I called she told me she had gone to the doctor because she cut herself while cutting a pan of brownies. I was worried and ask if I should come home and she assured me that she was fine. I worried for a while but then I heard that whisper from the Holy Spirit reminding me that I had promised to stay for five days.

That evening after dinner I went to bed early. I was reading the bible when I heard that whisper again say "Turn off the Light." I argued with God and said, "But I'm reading the bible!" I heard it again but even stronger. I turned out the light and saw what looked like the whole pasture on fire. I was scared and then I thought, what if I yell FIRE in a silent retreat center filled with people and there is no fire! I quickly slipped on my clothes and ran down the beautiful staircase.

I ran outside because I reasoned that if it were a fire I would see smoke and then I would scream. Well, there was no smoke! I ran back upstairs to the third-floor window. It was a stunning sunset that would take your breath away. It looked like something out of a science book with sunspots dancing across the palm trees and wooded pastures. It was so unobstructed and beautiful. Then I heard that whisper again say, "This is for you." It was so clear, and that moment changed my life. It gave me strength that I wasn't sure I had anymore. It gave me the gentle courage to keep going. It was twenty years ago and I think of it often. You have to be careful and discern where that small voice is coming from. I think the enemy was trying to trick me into going home and I would have missed one of the most beautiful encounters with God in my life. It gave me hope and the strength to keep going. I love the sunrise and sunsets even more than I did before. I have not shared this with a lot of people because I thought they would think I am a little, you know, but now I'm sharing it with everyone. Many times we must be careful who we share things with until God says it's time.

I had a special reassurance from God after my Mom had passed away. My oldest grandson Hunter was about 6 years old at the time. We were at the baseball field where he just finished up his season. All of the boys on his team were given helium balloons to celebrate. All of a sudden I saw Hunter let go of his balloon. I ask him why he had let it go. He told me he was letting it go to Grandma Mary in heaven. Oh my goodness. It was so sweet coming from this little baseball player.

The balloon was in the shape of a star. A little over a month later on the fourth of July my dad and some of our family were gathered on my parent's front porch. Every year we would watch the fireworks at dark from Lackland AFB and Seaworld and around the city. It was one of my Mom's favorite things and so it was difficult this first year without her. All of a sudden we saw a helium balloon just gently float down in front of us and land on the lawn. It was a silver star. I just paused for a moment and caught my breath and then I said "OK Mom, you are still with us, even though you are in heaven." It was amazing. It was another time that God blessed us with His presence. When my brother died about eight years before my Mom we all saw a beautiful rainbow a few days after his passing. There is an author that I love, SQuire Rushnell, that refers to these occurrences as GODwinks. I love that term.

There have been so many times that God sends a special message to give us strength. It can be a song that comes on the radio that is just perfect at that moment or a text from my children or friends. It can be a sweet hug from my husband or a grandchild. It can be an invitation to lunch from a friend or a quiet walk by the river. The stories written by Max Lucado have been a source of strength and God's Love for over twenty years. He makes the stories from the Bible so relatable. God's love comes in so many forms and through so many people. I participated in a Celebrate Recovery from Life's hurts and habits course about six years ago in San Antonio. I was given a spiritual companion during the process. It was a nine-month program. My spiritual companion, Patti, is still sending me inspiration and bible quotes to this day. That is a true gift from God!

God gave me a chance at marriage again. My husband Randy and I entered into this marriage with enough baggage to travel around the world. With God as the center of our lives we will make it. We were blessed to each have grandchildren when we met and have welcomed many more into the family since. There are many memories of God, Jesus, and the guidance of the Holy Spirit. One of our greatest gifts is to see our grown children and our grandchildren as they grow in their relationship with Our Heavenly Father.

This book is written to share my memories with you and to invite you to reflect on memories of your own. Please share those memories with someone you love.

I am so grateful.

I am grateful for Faith and Hope and Mercies that are new every day.

I know that Gentle Courage that comes from God will continue to grow for generations to come.

Blessings to you and yours!

Reflection page

_____

_____

_____

_____

_____

_____

_____

_____

_____

_____

_____

_____

_____

_____

Poetry

Written by Barbara Robbins-Ripps

Through the Years

This Poem was written during the Covid-19 Virus Pandemic which impacted our world in 2020. I wrote it to honor all who lost their lives to the virus.

Pandemic

I close my eyes in this quiet room
And my memories dance slowly by
Are you calling for me, or is it too soon
Lord, please sit with me as I silently cry

I try to remember when I first met you
My teacher said you will always be there
She showed us your love in that church pew
And said that you will always care

So today I know I am not alone
As I wait to see Your Light
Will I be a lucky one to recover and go home
Or will the careful hands of doctors and nurses continue to fight

Home in this world, or at Home with You
Whatever You will finally choose
It's okay whatever you want to do
Because in either home I will not lose

If I am reunited with my family here
Or prepare a place for them with You
I know all will cry a happy tear
For the touch of Your hand makes all things new.

Barbara Robbins-Ripps

May the Peace of Christ be with you all.

Reflection Page

_____

_____

_____

_____

_____

_____

_____

_____

_____

_____

_____

_____

_____

_____

_____

This poem was written at a time when I needed to call on God to help me through a rough time. I took a drive and saw an amazing Moonrise and I heard that whisper from our Heavenly Father say ~ KEEP YOUR EYES ON ME

God's Light in the Moon

The moon hangs high and full above
So bright and beautiful
Filled with God's Love
It's shining down and reaches me
A glimpse of God
It calms my soul, I reach back to see
So powerful and so strong
I need you now, and all day long

I pause, I sit, I pray to you
To take my heart and start anew
A joyful song, a happy smile
All for your good, each and every trial

The starlit sky, a gift from you
The sunrise and the sunset too
A breeze on one of the hottest days
They all are deserving of my praise

Because all good things, they come from you
And every promise and hope of something new
A butterfly dancing in the air
A little child without a care

Oh Jesus, thank you, for finding me
In all the corners that no one sees
I feel you close, I close my eyes
With mercies new, tomorrow I will rise.

Barbara Robbins-Ripps

Look forward to tomorrow, It will be a new day.

Reflection Page

This poem is written for my grandchildren.

I LOVE YOU TO THE MOON AND BACK!

Sweet Grandchildren

There is a sparkle in a grandchild's eye
A warmth in their sweet hug
There is laughter as they go buzzing by
And when they hurt your heartstrings tug

They treat you like a rock star
Run into your arms when you arrive
They can wrap you around their finger
And when you are blue they help you survive

They build forts with blankets everywhere
They love playing ball and having fun
So many years they live without a care
They grow too quickly like trees under the sun

I love hearing, watch what I can do
After 20 times you smile and say that's fine
Nana, I just learned this trick, it's new
Watch me Nana, just one more time

What a joy to watch your grandchild grow
That special love right from the start
What a blessing for a grandparent to know
A special love that fills your heart.

Barbara Robbins-Ripps

Reflection Page

This poem was written to share what Holy Eucharist means to me.

Holy Eucharist

The day you gave yourself to me
I was only seven years old
I came to you all dressed in white
And you were housed in a container of gold

A special teacher explained to me
How wonderful you are
She told us many stories
And I loved you from afar

I learned to see you in others
In their kindness and their love
I started searching for you in all things
And I felt many blessings from above

As the years went by my heart ached
On my journey life brought pain
But even in the tears and emptiness
Your presence brought sunshine in the rain

For a while, I felt so empty
My heart could feel no more
But you came to me in others
And you showed me one more door

I wait to spend time with you
When we are all alone
Your embrace has given me New Life
I no longer have a heart of stone

And now each week when you give yourself to me
It is just a tiny intricate part
Of your presence and your loving embrace
That I feel deep inside my heart

I no longer need a dress of white
And you a container of gold
You are with me each minute of every day
My best friend, the greatest possession I hold.

Barbara Robbins-Ripps

Reflection Page

_____

_____

_____

_____

_____

_____

_____

_____

_____

_____

_____

_____

_____

_____

I wrote this poem for an ACTS retreat team which was preparing for an upcoming retreat.

Be Still

Be still my child
Come rest with me
Close your eyes, calm your fears
See the dreams soon to be

Be still my child
I am the strength you need
I am the bread, blessed and broken
For the souls, we are to feed

Be still my child
There are many, yes I know
Look not only at the pain and sorrow
But the gift of Love we have to show

Be still my child
Feel my love and my embrace
Take the warmth that glows inside you
Share it, in my place

Be still my child
As you go forward, much to bear
Always remember you are never alone
Rest in me, I am always there

As the sunshine paints the morning sky
The stars shine softly through velvet blue
Go to speak and share with all you meet
My Love is given freely to empower YOU.

Barbara Robbins-Ripps

I wrote this poem after the completion of my Spiritual Director
Internship.

Reflection Page

_____

_____

_____

_____

_____

_____

_____

_____

_____

_____

_____

_____

_____

I wrote this poem after the completion of my Spiritual Director Internship.

Listen

Listen- as my breath
Travels deep inside my soul
Listen- God is reaching out
To embrace us, to make us whole

See a burning candle-
Feel Jesus present in the room
The sounds of soft chanting
Will be distant very soon

But they will always be remembered
And live deep within my heart
Though our bodies may grow distant
Our spirits will never part

For we have shared a sacred space
We have opened our hearts and cried many tears
We have prayed and laughed and prayed some more
We have slain dragons, and given names to our fears

We will always remain connected
What a precious gift I hold
Your shared faith, God's love, and your love
Your light travels with me
A gift so rare deep within my soul.

Barbara Robbins-RippsSDI 1996-1997

Reflection Page

This poem is dedicated to all victims of abuse.

Invisible

Tonight when you lay down your head
Imagine Christ embracing you
Because you have *never* been alone
He knows *everything* and will see you through

Each time that you felt no one cared
He felt your pain, he cried your tears
It seemed so long, it hurts so much
But He is there to calm your fears

You have *never* been invisible
For you are precious in His sight
He loves you and will fight for you
You are surrounded by His protective light

Stand firm, be strong
And trust in Him alone
Share your faith and empower others
Until he takes us all home.

Barbara Robbins-Ripps
Love and Prayers to all!

Reflection Page

I wrote this poem after watching a piece on the local news in January 2004 concerning beautiful religious statues being destroyed at San Fernando Cathedral in San Antonio, Texas. I was awakened by a whisper in the middle of the night prompting me to try to convey a message that has been heavy on my heart for a long time. I had prayed over and over for several years concerned about the heartbreaking abuse of individuals in our church. I knew that God would continue to reveal these terrible cases. This poem is written out of deep sadness but unceasing faith in Our Lord Jesus Christ.

When Jesus Wept

Today I felt such sadness, my heart began to weep
When a deeply hurting soul wandered into a sacred space
And shattered remembrances of Our Holy Family
A senseless crime he could not erase

As they interviewed the leaders of the Church
Their pain was evident, they wept and cried
It was so obvious their deep, sincere sadness
The regret and sorrow could not be denied

They called upon a master craftsman
Someone to put together every piece of stone
And my heart sank, and my breath left
If they only acted so quickly for our flesh and bone

There are many in our midst
They have been abused, shattered and torn
But they wait and fight to be heard and seen
Sometimes only to suffer others scorn

They find comfort in knowing that God knows all
But when day turns into night and they fall asleep
Jesus sees the pieces of broken hearts and lives everywhere
And I know that Jesus weeps

Please help heal and repair the broken lives
That has been entrusted to your care
The truth will set us free, God depends on you
God, our master craftsman is always there.

Barbara Robbins-Ripps

Reflection Page

_____

_____

_____

_____

_____

_____

_____

_____

_____

_____

_____

_____

_____

_____

This poem is written in loving memory of my brother Robert Samuel Robbins.

(August 19, 1957- January 19, 1997)

Wings

It was less than forty years ago
A young man was born so small and frail
He weighed a mere five pounds or so
A tiny cowboy, destined to blaze a trail

His roots grew deep in the country
His mom and dad both loved him so
They could not even imagine at the beginning
The special man they would come to know

They named this young man Robert
He learned to work, and ride, and pray
He would plan, and dream, and plan some more
Of all he wanted to be someday

Robie grew into a fine man
Fell in love, and married young
He kept dreaming and planning and building
And together with Barbara, they had two sons

He built his family a beautiful lake home
They would invite all the family and friends and more
Robie would drive his boat and take care of everyone
His heart and his home had an open door

Robie was a brave and strong cowboy
He rode bulls with spurs on his cuff

He loved the outdoors and fishing and hunting
Always wore boots and a cap and in his
pocket a can of Copenhagen snuff

He built a business because like his father
Robie wanted roots for his family
With hard work, sweat, and determination
Many of his dreams had already come to be

His age was not yet forty
An untimely death he would now see
But not without giving wings to his sons
And special memories to his wife, friends, and family

So now this Big Man has a place in Heaven
At this hour a choir of Angels will sing western swing
The swinging doors of heaven have now opened
FOR A BIG TEXAS COWBOY WITH WINGS.

Barbara Robbins-Ripps

Reflection Page

This poem was written in loving memory of my mother, Mary Robbins.

Mary

Mary always loved her family
To her they meant everything
From a little girl to wife, mother, and grandma
Her love surrounds us like heaven's ring

Mary loved taking care of her husband
They still would regularly disagree
A stubborn nature was passed down to us all
From our beloved Mary, Mary quite contrary

She often had a quick-witted comment
To make us laugh or sometimes blush
Mary always had a twinkle in her eyes
That even Alzheimer's couldn't crush

Mary made holidays so very special
Her home decorated beautifully for all to see
Everything was carefully done to perfection
From the meal, the cookies, to the Christmas tree

Mary took special pride in her children and grandchildren
She loved to watch them run and laugh and play
She went to games and school programs as they grew
And most important she taught them to always pray

Are you making them smile up in heaven
Because we miss you so much down here
But you are with us every step of the way
And in our hearts, we will always hold you dear

So keep watching over our family
Heaven's angel with a twinkle in her eye
We will do our best to make you proud of us all
Until we meet again in the newly decorated home in the sky.

Barbara Robbins-Ripps

Reflection Page

_____

_____

_____

_____

_____

_____

_____

_____

_____

_____

_____

_____

_____

_____

I wrote this poem two years after my mother passed away. I wrote it on Mother's Day in her memory.

Beyond

There are no words to verbalize
All that is in my heart today
So I will float through images and memories
And try to express them in some unorganized way

A velvet black night sky
Filled with twinkling light, that takes my breath away
Your presence, your eyes quietly upon me
In every dance, routine, or event that came my way.

Love from a Mother, love to a child
Love is given freely that reaches the sky
It travels back again, it is multiplied
It has grown beyond substance, to spirit, it sours and flies

In the breezes, you can feel it
In the celebrations, you can see
The eyes of family, friends, and of the children
The way she began, and always meant for it to be

Share all you have seen and learned from her
Whether years many or a few
The gift of a child or a mother
Expands love exchanged in all you will ever do

Remember the laughter, remember the fun
Remember the embraces and even some of the rain
Because we not only loved each other in the good times
It grew deeper in our challenges and the rain

Beyond words, beyond time
Beyond your strength - to the divine
Beyond your memories, beyond mine
Close in the heart - forever shine.

Barbara Robbins-Ripps

Reflection Page

_____

_____

_____

_____

_____

_____

_____

_____

_____

_____

_____

_____

_____

_____

This poem is written in loving memory of my Great-Aunt Gladys Kriewald.

Aunt Gladys

There is a family that you see on Holidays
Aunt Gladys was much much more
She was close to my Dad and Mom
We went on vacation. fishing, and had fun galore

We had a place at Medina Lake
We would swim, and fish, and play
There were great meals prepared and shared outside
And campfire smores at the end of the day

Our family often stayed a week or so
Aunt Gladys taught us card games and how to cook
She would laugh and joke and have so much fun
When running the trotlines we would
catch a whopper on the hook

The memories live on through time
Even though she has been gone for so many years
Our children and grandchildren enjoy this special place
They are making new memories, no time for tears

So, thank you from the bottom of our hearts
Daddy is still keeping the memories going
Your fishing trips, family fun, and lake memories
In our campfires will forever be glowing.

Barbara Robbins-Ripps

Reflection Page

This poem is written in the loving memory of my grandmother Lora Robbins.

Omie

Lora was a farm girl
A hard worker her whole life
As a young girl, she picked cotton
Living through the depression and great strife

Grandma made us feel so special
In her little country home up on the hill
Sitting on her quiet screened-in porch
The smell of homemade cookies lingered still

She would wrap them up to give away
Take them to family and friends
It was homemade love in her own way
To share sweet love that never ends

The great-grandchildren called her Omie
A greeting from tender and worn German hands
The children would play in the yard under the shade tree
With spoons, old dishes and pots, and pans

Her bible always on the kitchen table
Highlighted and written in, used and worn
Oh how precious the sign of her strong faith
Passed on to others forevermore

There stands a church on the family land
And many homes fill acres on the hill
The family farm a great heritage to pass on hand to hand
Families making precious memories not only today but forever will

Barbara Robbins-Ripps

Reflection Page

This poem was written in loving memory of my Grandmother Clarise Keller-Elmendorf.

Carry on

Grandma was a strong woman
Clarise was there for everyone
Her career as a nurse was exemplary
She gave her all until the day was done

The doctors that worked alongside her
Said "She taught me all I know"
They would smile at the mention of her name
Santa Rosa hospital was sad to see her go

Her rosary at her bedside
She would light candles and always pray
For all the members of her family
The many intentions of all every day

Her husband had passed away forty years ago
She told me stories of their younger years
I can see him waiting at heaven's gate
With a handful of carnations and happy tears

I can hear her saying carry on
Look after every one
I will watch over you in heaven
Look for me each day in the rising sun

Barbara Robbins-Ripps

Reflection Page

_____

_____

_____

_____

_____

_____

_____

_____

_____

_____

_____

_____

_____

_____

This poem was written for Tori Bippert who died tragically in a car accident at the age of 16.

Tori

She is the new color in the rainbow
The new star in the night sky
The sweet scent that passes when the wind blows
The smile of a stranger as they walk by

She is the strength you need this morning
Your strength in all the days ahead
The lovely sound as the church bells ring
The sleep at night when you rest your head

She is the reason to be strong today
The arms of every friend
The love you have cannot be broken
It will last for eternity, it will never end

She is the bright colors in the sunrise
Cheering us on as we live each day
Standing beside Jesus in the blue skies
Shining her light in just her sweet way

She is the hope for tomorrow
She is the faith in God we share
She is the comfort in our sorrow
She is, and always will be there.

Barbara Robbins-Ripps

Reflection Page

This poem was written in memory of Joey Resendez who took his own life as a teenager. It was written from the thoughts and memories of close friends.

Our Prayer for Joey

Joey~ you are not forgotten
You are with us every day
Always to be remembered
A part of our hearts you'll always stay

Joey~ always made us laugh
He cared for everyone
He gave good advise, did not criticize
In his smile, we saw the sun

Jen and Joey in Spanish class
Teacher's pets their friends would say
Passing notes and just talking
That's the way they would spend their day

Cathy, Michael, Zach, and Eric
Would pick Joey up at noon
They were family and very close friends
And very hurt that it ended so soon

Your cousin Joey will always remember
The special friendship that you shared
The way you always listened
The way you always cared

Joey~ gave so much you see
He cared more for others than for himself
He took Josh for walks, was a faithful friend
Sometimes leaving his feelings on a shelf

We pray for you every day
And as our graduation nears
We know that your spirit is with us
We will try to wipe away our tears

Because knowing you was a blessing
And for you, we will do our best
To show love the way that you did
And let God take care of the rest.

Barbara Robbins-Ripps

Reflection Page

_____

_____

_____

_____

_____

_____

_____

_____

_____

_____

_____

_____

_____

This poem was written for a young girl who struggled with mental issues and self- acceptance.

Mandy

As I sit and think so quietly
Of the world, I've come to know
A lovely young lady dances through my mind
I've had the honor of watching grow

She has a heart so tender and caring
One that has been touched by pain
So much like Jesus, she tries to give her best
And Mandy is her name

This world is not always kind
So many obstacles to bear
But Mandy, know that you are not alone
Those who love you will always be there

May each day bring you much closer
To realize how very special YOU are
May you find happiness in each sunrise
You are a light brighter than a star

Know that life is not going to be easy
Jesus told us that from the start
Have faith that he is always there
He lives within your heart

Mandy, have a beautiful day
Take one precious moment at a time
Knowing that you are loved, and with Jesus at your side
There is no mountain you cannot climb

TODAY IS A NEW BEGINNING
KNOW THAT GOD LOVES YOU,
JUST THE WAY YOU ARE
GIVE YOUR CARES AND CONCERNS
TO HIM EACH DAY
HE BELIEVES IN YOU AND IS
WATCHING YOU FROM AFAR.

Barbara Robbins-Ripps

Reflection Page

_____

_____

_____

_____

_____

_____

_____

_____

_____

_____

_____

_____

_____

_____

This poem was written in memory of a family friend, Edgar Skolaut, who lost his battle with cancer.

A Letter to Edgar

I remember many years ago
When I was just a girl
We would go to visit the Skolaut house
And things were always in a whirl

Junior was in trouble again, way on top of the roof
Edgar shouted "You come down from there"
But knowing what was in store for him
Of course he did not dare!

Elvira was in the kitchen
The smell of cinnamon rolls filled the air
Her cooking was the very best
There were goodies everywhere

Doug was in the back yard
Playing football, dodging trees
Jackie playing with Mrs. Beasley
Just as sweet as you please

My family always had a good time
The parents sat around the kitchen table
The boys played shoes and football
And I would read Jackie an Aesop fable

Well we all grew up, we all stayed friends
The children married too
We loved to fish, to hunt, and eat
And to tell jokes, Edgar had a few

At the camp house at Wurzbach ranch
There were Pearl beer, a little hunting and a lot of cards
The deer were always safe there
To be shot they had to wander in the yard

We had a lot of good times
The memories are all great
With Edgar as the Commander in Chief
The parties would all rate

So Edgar, we would like to say,
we thank you from the start,
You truly are a dear friend,
and a special person from the heart.

Barbara Robbins-Ripps

Reflection Page

This poem was written in memory of my aunt, Helen Hawkins, who died from lung cancer.

Helen

It seems the heavens opened up
To take you and your family
A beautiful rainbow left a promise
That we would meet again for eternity

Time took on a whole new meaning
When you and others were filled with pain
We didn't want to lose you
But in dying you were healed, never to hurt again

You raised six wonderful children
It wasn't easy, so much to do
Your day began at three or four in the morning
It was your job, they all depended on you

With the support of your strong-willed mother
You gained a strength that all could see
No one can understand all the challenges
Only our God sees the inside of you and me

There are children and grandchildren
So beautiful and so strong
They are a testament to your life here
They will carry your memory their whole life long

Grandma Helen went to games and cheered them on
You knitted blankets and made special meals
You sat with some in deep long-suffering
And your courage let them know your love was real

When heaven opened up you were greeted
by Our Mother Mary, your Mom and sisters too
you embraced your son and helped him through his journey
to join our Lord, his family, and you

We will carry on like those before us
we will miss you but we know
that our job is to care for the family left here
watch over them all until they grow.

Barbara Robbins-Ripps

Reflection Page

This poem was written in memory of my cousin, Ben Yancy Jr. Ben had received a liver transplant and passed on before reaching the age of 50.

Ben

Ben has arrived in heaven
And he did it his own way
A biker rode in through heavens gates
To Jesus open arms and smiles on this reunion day

His mother was there to make this passage
From life on earth to eternal life above
A journey that was not one of doubt or fear
But of excitement to the light of a mothers love

Ben was blessed in this life with Cindy
A loving wife of deep devotion
They clung to each other with a deep faith
This love will continue to flow deeper than any ocean

Because a love like this is never-ending
The children and grandchildren left behind
Will grow and carry on the love that they began
And it will be everlasting, defeating time

He leaves his dad, a brother, sisters and friends
And in heaven joins the rest of his family
To prepare a place for us when God calls us home
No pain or worries, we will come together and all be free

So rest easy now with Jesus
Our biker Angel at heaven's door
We will miss you but we find comfort
Knowing you're our protector until we meet once more.

Barbara Robbins-Ripps

Reflection Page

_____

_____

_____

_____

_____

_____

_____

_____

_____

_____

_____

_____

_____

_____

This poem was written in loving memory of my Uncle, Emil (Buzzy) Elmendorf.

A Tribute to Buzzy Elmendorf

It was early Monday evening
As I sat quietly in my chair
A large white dove fluttered by my window
And then circled back again, making sure I knew he was there

I quickly ran over to the window
Trying to see him one more time
But he was gone ~ as quickly as he came
A beautiful gift, a heavenly sign

He seemed to say, I'm on my way now
I just flew by to say good-bye
The dove was strong and soaring boldly
Out of sight, lifted to the skies

When I heard the news the next morning
A new meaning was revealed by that dove
I knew his spirit was already flying
And he said good-byes to all he loved

His loving and committed wife Pat, Aaron and Blaine the fine
two sons, he raised to be strong
Becky and Yvette his loving daughter- in-
laws helped the family grow
Their beautiful grandchildren Kaeleigh, Drew, and Evan
They all made him so proud his face would glow

He was hard-working, a true craftsman
A hunter, a loving uncle, and a loyal and good friend

He could build a home, a hot rod car, truck and more
His talent shared each day lives on, never to end

It was time to rest, to take a break, but
we know he will not rest long
With his father and mother, sisters and family
He will be preparing a place for us all
So lift your eyes to the stars, find comfort in God and each other
And hold your memories dear until we hear his call.

Barbara Robbins-Ripps

Reflection Page

I wrote this poem while taking a class at the Chancery in the 1990s.

Moral Tradition

Jesus, it is you that I turn to in my prayer
Jesus, It is in you that I always find someone to care
Jesus, long before you prophecies began to unfold
All of God's beautiful lessons of the values we are to hold

God came to rescue Israel
To show his loving ways
The path we are to take
For life in truth to stay

We are called to remembrance
To remember all God's laws
We are called to recognize injustice
And closer to you we must always draw

Jesus, with you God sent a message
That the law alone was not enough
That on the spirit of the law we must rely upon
Even though our road will be rough

Jesus, in memory of you
Our vision truly expands
By your example of compassion to your enemies, to sinners
And to people of all lands.

Jesus, in your presence, with your guidance
Help me to see you in all things
Help me to show your love to others
It is only in loving you and sharing you
That we find the happiness you bring

Jesus, it is in thanking you
That I end my humble prayer
For your loving embrace to all people
For me, you are always there

Barbara Robbins-Ripps

Reflection Page

This poem is written in loving memory of Beaujames Loosmore
July 10, 1977 – May 23, 2020

Beaujames

There is a bright new smile in heaven
A new shining star in the velvet sky
A new gamer rearranging starlight
Painting new colors in the sunsets from up high

There is new music for Julie and Evie
In the soft coastal breezes that now blow
There are reminders in the songs that they play
Beaujames unending love they will always know

Joining your family that have gone before you
To your mom, sisters, family, and friends
There is a promise from God of eternal life
The circle never broken, the love never ends

Are you planning a feast in heaven?
A celebration where we are all together in God's Light
Where the music, and colors, and the love that surrounds us
Is all peaceful, beautiful, and so bright

Please watch over us new angel Beaujames
With that infectious smile, and love, and grace
Prepare a place for us to join you again
United in heaven, in Jesus loving embrace.

Barbara Robbins-Ripps

Reflection Page

This poem was written for my oldest grandson as he ventured out in the world to live on his own. I pray for all my grandchildren as they move into adulthood. You are never alone! God is with you always!

True Freedom

Looking forward, always upward
As you lean into this life-
No day will be without challenges
Many happy moments, and sometimes strife

But one thing you can always count on
Is that God is always there
Standing with you, right beside you
Jesus arms outstretched, all your burdens he will bare

From your sparkling eyes as a baby
To a barefoot boy running free and fast
There was always a dream deep down inside you
Every step of the way you can't get passed

There is a deep love from all your family
Fragmented but whole it always stands
Everyone praying each day for you
For your future that is in God's hands

God sees when you are in trouble
And he says "Look, I'm right here"
He has plans for a great life for you
He reveals His miracles - your path to clear

Live in gratitude for second chances
For His saving Grace and Love
Live in awe of His mighty presence

Always stay connected to the one above

For there is no greater power
He will lead you to where you should be
No greater love each and every hour
Hang on tight, He will set you free.

To Hunter
Love, Nana
2018

GODSPEED

Reflection Page

Afterword

I want to say thank you to the reader for spending this time with me. I have written this book for my family and friends but I pray it reaches others as well. Living in this unpredictable time facing the Covid-19 Virus makes us truly realize each day is a gift and we are never sure of a tomorrow. We knew that already but in isolation we see it so much clearer. I hope you were able to use the reflection pages to focus on your journey and walk with God.

In this book I tried to focus on the power of God in our lives. I did not go into detail of all the challenges I have faced and the choices I have made that caused pain. In your life I know you will be faced with many challenges and choices that are very difficult. My prayer is that you reach out to God first in prayer and then to someone you trust to help to guide you.

I have a close friend that shared a very special spiritual experience with me the other day. She told me she would only share it with me and one other because some people may think it wasn't real or that she thinks she is special that God revealed himself to her in such a beautiful way. I just want to say that YOU are special. ALL OF YOU! YOU ARE A CHILD OF GOD! I know it is hard to share deeply spiritual experiences with others at times. Look at Mary Magdalene, the apostles, and on and on. There will be the right time and the right person. We just have to pray for God's direction. Each of us is different. God reveals himself to us in different ways. He gives us different gifts and talents to use in His honor. That is what makes the world a beautiful place. I wish I could sing! That is not one of the gifts that God blessed me with. I am grateful to the ones who have that gift and share it with others. I love music and it makes my world so much better.

My prayer is that you use your gifts. Whatever they may be, use them for the Glory of God. You can use them in your homes, in your schools, in your workplace, in your favorite sport, everywhere.

I can do all this through him who gives me strength.

Philippians 4:13 NIV

When I was a little girl I remember the teacher asking the typical question, "What do you want to do when you grow up?" My answer was "I want to make a difference."

May God Bless you on your journey and may you make a difference one life at a time.

Love and Prayers,
Barbara (Mom, Nana)
Praise God!

Printed in the United States
By Bookmasters